CW00545922

HOPE FOR ADVENT

ADVENT REFLECTIONS

SUSAN SAYERS

kevin
mayhew

First Published in 2022 by Kevin Mayhew Ltd,

Fengate Farm,

Rattlesden,

Bury St Edmunds,

Suffolk, IP30 0SZ

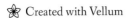 Created with Vellum

CONTENTS

INTRODUCTION

WHAT CHILD IS THIS?

Introduction: before you begin

Advent is a season in its own right. It's also the start of the entire Christian year. So how can we best honour it?

We honour it by using it! It is the season which marks the start of the Christian year, so this is our opportunity to reflect on who on Earth the child is – not only in the manger, but throughout his life, and throughout our own lives, too. It's also a season to be lived in the dark. Light is promised but it's important to pay attention to the darkness as well.

This Advent book is a kind of travel guide or maybe a theatre programme. You may be visiting familiar places and ideas, or places and ideas you haven't previously considered in quite the same way. You might be surprised to find our Advent journey linking with other seasons, so it isn't entirely about getting ready for Christmas.

I can't promise you an entirely comfortable journey, but I hope it will be a journey that helps you travel through this coming year, on your own life pilgrimage, equipping you with hope in the darkness, whatever form that darkness takes for you.

As there are four weeks in the Advent season, this book is in four sections. In each section there is a weekly prayer, then six short daily reflections, followed by suggestions for you to try. So as we journey through Advent there are questions to think about, suggested further reflection and action.

May God bless us as we journey together.

Week 1: Into the darkness

Week 2: Prequels

Week 3: Cast list

Week 4: Curious hope

WEEK 1: INTO THE DARKNESS

This week's prayer:

***You may find it helpful to pray this prayer
each day for the first week in Advent***

Holy One
In this Advent season of the year
I come to you empty handed
But ready to receive;
Give me enough humility
To be honest,
And enough faith
To respond to your gentle guidance.
May I never forget
How tenderly you love me.
Amen.

DAY 1

Reflection for Week 1, Day 1

All around us the Advent calendars are being opened, the Christmas cards and messages sent, the trees bought and decorated, and the excitement or dread building.

And where are we? Maybe slightly dislocated as we attempt to do both Christmas and Advent at the same time? Maybe stressed and overworked, or grieving the loss of a job, or even a loved one? Maybe anxious about the future or the finances, maybe hoping for a more normal Christmas this year?

It's quite encouraging to find that Luke's gospel doesn't start with the imminent birth of Jesus, but with an ageing and very sceptical priest. He's still going through the priestly rituals as usual, but the cry of his heart is powerful. His darkness, his grief, is being childless. And God does not yet seem to have answered his prayer.

The priest's name is Zachariah and, like all of us, there is darkness in his life as well as the hope of light.

Try this...

- You have probably heard and read it often before, but perhaps now is the time to read it slowly and afresh. It's the beginning of St Luke's Gospel, and at this beginning of the Christian year, I wonder what the Holy Spirit will nudge you to notice as you read?
- Don't plunge into the reading though. Spend a moment completely still – as still as the walls around where you are sitting. You are sitting at the feet of Jesus, ready to listen.
- And now you can read Luke, chapter 1, verses 5-25.

DAY 2

Reflection for Week 1, Day 2

The first thing I want us to consider is that Advent is a season of darkness, as well as promise. This child, born of Mary, has actually come to share in our darkness as well as in our glimpses of light. Rather than banishing our darkness and replacing it with light, the coming of God into the whole reality of creation shows us a far more generous and loving reality. The God of Light loves us so much that sharing our darkness is a central part of this extraordinary venture.

And what does that mean for us?

Well, it means that we don't need to pretend the darkness isn't there in our own lives. Pretending won't make it disappear in any case. Advent is not a time to fix our jaws into a smile as we crank up the demands for Christmas preparation. Through Zachariah Luke reminds us that being in tune with our own particular areas of darkness is OK. In fact, it has much to teach us about who this Christmas child really is.

Try this...

- I know you were reading this passage yesterday, but try reading it again today. Use the same method and remember to be attentive as you read.
- It's Luke chapter 1 verses 5-25.

DAY 3

Reflection for Week 1, Day 3

You may prefer to engage with this reflection in the company of someone you trust. Please be gentle with yourself.

I wonder if Zachariah blurted out his pain and disappointment (of being childless) to the angel, because the good news Gabriel brought was just too impossibly good for him to believe or cope with.

It is as if his original hope for a child has over the years hardened into resignation, and now into the bitter, painful truth that due to his age and his wife's being past the menopause, his hope is hopeless, and there can never be a child. Gabriel's message that he and Elizabeth are to be parents after all, perhaps felt to Zachariah as if salt was being rubbed into the raw wound of his deep unspoken grief?

. . .

We as all humans, often do the same. If an original bright hope we once had is never realised, it can harden over time into resignation, heartache and cynicism, and that is a real, painful darkness which we carry with us into every place and every relationship.

Let's begin this Advent journey by doing something which takes quite a lot of courage. I wonder if we can be honest enough to acknowledge any areas of darkness that live in our hearts right now. They may be linked with the current state of our world, or they may be personal. Spend just a few minutes acknowledging these areas of darkness.

I'm not suggesting you need to stay in this place, but we do need to recognise where we hurt and where there is heartache, even if we only glance at it from the corner of our eye. You can be reassured that it will never be increased by you acknowledging it; but by doing so, your self-honesty has increased, and with it the real possibility of healing, or even transforming.

But here is the news of comfort and joy: Whatever else the child in the Christmas manger is, this child is none other than the One who has chosen to join us where we really are – in the darkness we all truly inhabit but often ignore, hiding its painful truth even from ourselves. Perhaps it is so dangerously painful that we banish it and never speak or think of it.

Advent is not so much about darkness turned into light; it's more about an extraordinary reality – light choosing to live *within* our darkness.

Try this...

- Notice the darkness revealed in everyday life, in the news.
- Go for a walk by yourself, turn off your phone, or even perhaps turn off the light and sit in darkness for a few minutes.
- Read once again the conversation between Zachariah and Gabriel.
- Read also Psalm 113 verse 5.

DAY 4

Reflection for Week 1, Day 4

But why on earth do we have to become explorers of painful darkness during this pre-Christmas season? Surely we should be filled with joyful anticipation? I'll try and explain.

We have evolved within a spinning and orbiting planet habitat. In the ancient description of the beginning, in the first book of the bible – Genesis – there is the darkness of chaos until the Creator speaks light into existence. We might puzzle over the light being created before the sun, moon and stars. And we now know that our planet Earth was spinning through darkness and light long before there was even any life here.

Yet what scientists are now beginning to discover is that at the start of the whole universe there was indeed darkness until the first stars exploded into light. Our own, much later, local light and darkness is simply due to the way our planet home spins, facing alternately towards and away from our nearest star.

But since our eyesight developed on this planet to be as useful as possible during daylight, we humans have often felt more vulnerable in the darkness of night. Whether lighting fires at the entrance of our caves, or switching on street lighting in our towns and cities, we have always done our best to turn night into day. In fact it's only recently, with the aid of efficient night vision cameras, that we have been able to see and marvel at all the rich life that goes on in the dark, and of which we were previously unaware.

The great cost of all this artificial light, however, is that light pollution now prevents us from seeing all the other stars! We have to designate 'dark places' to visit as tourists to the kingdom of night. And when we visit, we discover how darkness enables us to see light – thousands of lights – as we gaze at the sky. Even though it has become a metaphor for anything sinister, dangerous, fearful or downright terrifying, the truth is that darkness has great value.

Try this...

- Dress warmly and step out into the darkness. Yes, it may well be too cloudy to see any stars, and it might be wet! Do it anyway.
- Look up and readjust your focus until you realise you are not really looking 'up' at all, but DEEP. Out, into the rest of the universe. You are a space traveller and the point on your planet spaceship where you are standing is facing away from the sun.

DAY 5

Reflection for Week 1, Day 5

Advent provides us with a passport to visit a profoundly 'dark place'. Our Advent journey is leading us away from well-lit city streets and Christmas lights, out into the dark where our eyesight is far less effective, and where we realise our vulnerability. But this very darkness reveals the lights of other stars, which our own close star drowns out during daylight. We need to enter darkness to catch sight of the heavens.

Interestingly, the child of Bethlehem was born, not in daylight but during the night. And during this Advent season, we too are experiencing darkness (in the northern hemisphere) so that we can better catch sight of the child of Light being born into the dark; into our human dark. As Zachariah realised, 'In the tender compassion of our God the dawn from on high shall break upon us, to shine on those *who dwell in darkness and the shadow of death.*' Luke 1.78-79

. . .

We are deliberately recognising that we do dwell in darkness, and the shadow of death, both personal and universal, both in its aching laments, and in our fearful vulnerability. We do this so as to experience the way it teaches us so much about light and enlightenment. It's not a make-believe fairy story where there is always a happy ending. We all know that happy endings are sometimes in short supply, and we have to learn the hard rocky path of offering our very darkness to God, knowing that God can always bring about some kind of blessing and transformation, impossible as that may seem.

Try this...

- Walk round a churchyard and read some of the headstones. Become aware of the temporary nature of this life, and our family links with those have lived and died. Be thankful for the precious, fragile gift of life. Be thankful for each moment.
- Pray for those who dwell in a particularly terrifying darkness at the moment, standing alongside them in your heart and soul.
- Read Genesis 1.1-2. Read it slowly and attentively. Several times!

DAY 6

Reflection for Week 1, Day 6

I've said that darkness, though not necessarily the most comfortable place for us, is of great value to us, as it enables us to see and notice distant lights, like stars. And another thing about darkness is the way it enables us to engage with one another. Think, for instance, of gathering around a fire at night. Much of our scriptures would have been handed down through the generations by the stories told around a fire. Perhaps you can remember camp fire songs sung in the darkness. With huge night all around, people feel close and comforted by gathering in the light and warmth of a fire, and in this relaxed place, there can be sharing which might not happen in the full light of day.

People are often less embarrassed about speaking of deep feelings when the lights are low. Dwelling in darkness, then, can help us listen and encourage us to feel our connectedness, not only within our fractured selves but also with one another and with God our Heavenly Father.

Perhaps this Advent is an opportunity for us to change our thinking about darkness, recognising it for what it is both without and within, and feeling more powerfully than ever the affectionate love God has for each of us. A love so strong that it spills out through a human birth to share the full reality of real life here. Messy, confusing, damaging, fearful, and disappointing. Our darkness as well as our light.

Try this…

- Read Luke chapter 1, verses 57-80.
- Light a candle and turn off the lights, making sure you do this safely!
- Sit still. Completely still.
- Notice the shadows, the light and the darkness. In all of it God's love is here and in every place and time.

WEEK 2: PREQUELS

This week's prayer:

***You may find it helpful to pray this prayer
each day during the second week in Advent***

Holy and promised One,
I join those walking to Emmaus
As I listen to you this week.
May my heart burn within me
As I discover more and more
Of your love.
More and more
Of all the costly loving that led
To the manger and the cross.
Amen.

DAY 1

Reflection for Week 2, Day 1

We have seen how Zachariah, as he held his baby son, was finally able to speak again, after his encounter with Gabriel, and once the promised child was born and named.

We can feel his relief, joy and amazement as he prophesies real hope for all who 'dwell in darkness and the shadow of death'. The birth of his own son, which had seemed utterly impossible, has clinched for him the truth of God's tender compassion, so that he can now speak out with complete conviction.

And what about Mary? Even before Mary's child has been born, the identity of her child is proclaimed as 'the mighty Saviour', through whom God comes to his people and sets them free. Zachariah is able to give a bit of the back story even before we reach the manger. He knows that this child to be born will belong to the house, or family, of the great King David, so Joseph is also included.

With any story or film we always like to watch the prequel – to discover the real beginning of our heroes! And this week we are going to discover some of the prophecies written long before Jesus was born. Zachariah is one of the last. But what else was seen by the seers?

To find out we need to take a journey back in time, and read from ancient documents. This week we become Advent Archaeologists, sifting carefully to unearth hints and fragments which can tell us more about the child still hidden, still being knit together in Mary's womb.

Try this...

- Read (in the same way as before) Luke chapter 24, verses 13-27.

DAY 2

Reflection for Week 2, Day 2

When the risen Christ joined those two disciples on their way home to Emmaus from Jerusalem, Jesus took them on a whistle stop tour of the Jewish scriptures, reminding them of all the passages which predicted his own life, even including the suffering of his torture and death. Not that his lesson ended there. After all, this wasn't a ghost who had joined them. Jesus was explaining to them how the scriptures had made it clear that the Messiah – the Anointed One – would have to suffer before he entered again into glory.

It isn't recorded which scriptures passages Jesus used, but there are certainly many to choose from. Think of Genesis – the book of origins – for example. The whole drama of the scriptures is presented here at the beginning in the powerful story of ourselves and our relationship with God the creator. It tells of the human propensity to want to better ourselves, to be independent of our Maker, to go our own way rather than God's way. This is, if you like, our Achilles heel. Having been gifted Free Will, so that we are enabled to love by free choice, we are constantly abusing this gift, choosing self-centeredly, rather than lovingly.

As the risen Jesus patiently explains to these two disciples, all scripture points to the only possible way of real healing and liberation for us. The Messiah, as both human and divine, will have to suffer because his love never ever stops. Love is the entirety of his meaning.

Try this...

- Read Genesis, chapter 3, verses 1-24. It's quite a lengthy story, but a very important one.
- Read it understanding how it is our human story. Adam and Eve represent all of us and our relationship with our loving Creator.

DAY 3

Reflection for Week 2, Day 3

We always prefer good news to uncomfortable or challenging news. And yet we well know that there are times when we have grown stronger or wiser through challenges we have had to face. Sometimes those who have never been challenged have less understanding either of themselves or others.

When Jesus joined those two disciples he wanted to explain to them something very important about the promised Messiah, which they had missed. Maybe it had been sidelined as people preferred to home in on the many prophecies about the expected Messiah setting them free from oppression. Since they were living in a time when their Roman occupation left the Jewish people with only very circumscribed freedom, it's no wonder they had forgotten this less comfortable but central part of the Messiah's mission. Notice what the Emmaus disciples had hoped Jesus would be. (in verses 19-21)

It's clear that dying through a cursed execution was certainly not how they had imagined the Messiah's mission to end.

Yet as their unrecognised companion reminded them, the prophet Isaiah had spelt out what would be a necessary part of Messiah's work; necessary, yes, but to many, completely unthinkable. The Messiah would have to undergo acute suffering and rejection before entering into glory.

Although we are on an Advent pilgrimage, we also need to recognise how closely linked are the Christmas manger and the Good Friday cross. Searching the prequel to the manger leads us to a better understanding.

Try this...

- Read Isaiah chapter 53, verses 1-12
- As you read these words, imagine the risen Jesus joining you on your walk, and reminding you of this prophecy, which refers to himself.

DAY 4

Reflection for Week 2, Day 4

We are journeying through this Advent season with Mary and Joseph
as they travel to the City of Bread: Beth-le-hem. They carry with
them a very special load. It is Mary's unborn child, the son foretold
by the prophets, the son who would be the Messiah, God-with-Us,
Emmanu-el. The Messiah's purpose is to be God with us. Not only
his purpose, prophesied by Ezekiel and told by Gabriel to Mary at the
annunciation, but also his name has been told to Joseph, who is
himself a descendant of King David. And the city of Bethlehem is the
city where King David was born and raised, as a shepherd boy. The
child is to be named Yeshua. We know that name as Jesus, but as you
can see, it was significant, since Joshua (another form of Yeshua) had
been the one to lead God's people into the promised land, as Moses'
successor. Into freedom from slavery.

· · ·

So we begin to see that this Christmas baby in the manger did not suddenly appear from nowhere, but had been foretold in so many different ways for hundreds of years. Understand the Prequel and you better understand the way Jesus the Christ is the culmination of God's great loving plan.

He will be born in King David's city, he will be the Good Shepherd and he will lead God's people into freedom. He will be 'God with us', the visible image of the unseen God. As the Christ/Messiah (the anointed One) this baby will grow up to reveal God's faithful love for us all, in the language of a human life, whether we humans accept him or reject him. It is both necessary and inevitable, then, that there will be rejection, misunderstanding, anguish and terrible suffering precisely so that God's complete loving can be shown to be without any get-out clauses or small print. God's loving never runs out. Never.

Try this...

- Here are some other references which you can look up in your bible.
- Deuteronomy 18.15 and 43.10-11, Isaiah 42.6, Isaiah 49.6, Ezekiel 34.11-12 and 23, Zechariah 12.10Malachi 3.1, Micah 5.2-4. Psalms 22, 23.
- Any of them might have been part of what Jesus used to explain to the despairing disciples on their way to Emmaus about what we are exploring as the Prequel to the baby in the manger, the young man being executed by crucifixion, and the resurrected Christ joining them on the road.

DAY 5

Reflection for Week 2, Day 5

One way of exploring the Prequel to Jesus the Christ, is to join the Advent archeological dig through the scriptures (what we know as the Old Testament). And that's what we have been doing, along with many other curious theologians.

Another way is to 'dig' in the gospel accounts of Jesus. When I first began investigating various things Jesus said, by exploring the cross-referencing others had kindly provided, I was quite stunned by how many of Jesus's words and actions were actually fulfilled quotations from the scriptures. So, metaphorically, we have an archaeological trench already dug, and all we need to do is come with our trowels and old toothbrushes to uncover the finds!

. . .

The fact that Jesus quotes the scriptures so much, immediately shows us something about this Christmas baby and his life now starting to unfold. As he grew up he must have been immersed in the writings of these scrolls. We know from Luke's gospel that at twelve years old he spent several days in the temple at Jerusalem listening and asking questions. (Luke 2.41-49) It's likely that Mary and Joseph would also have helped him learn and question and understand. Maybe he also helped his brothers and sisters, as siblings often do. And he was only six months younger than John the baptiser. They may well have talked things over together.

Without the luxury of printed books, much of the learning would have been memory work. This is a method we have largely disregarded since our devices and AI are so much easier and quicker. But it's worth a try. Start perhaps with a verse of a psalm. The advantage of memorising by heart is that we always have those words with us. Monks and nuns were once expected to learn all the psalms by heart so they could recite them as they worked and walked! For many of us, the daily prayer at morning and evening allow the psalms to soak into our hearts and minds.

Try this...

- Think of all the words of scripture you already know by heart, such as favourite psalms, words used during worship, the Lord's prayer... and maybe add others.
- Look up these cross-references so you can see how Jesus is rooted in the scriptures:
- 1) Matthew 4.4 and Deuteronomy 8.3
- 2) Matthew 4.7 and Deuteronomy 6.16
- How well do we know the scriptures?

DAY 6

Reflection for Week 2, Day 6

Yesterday we cross-referenced some of the first reported words of
Jesus. How useful it was for him to know those quotations by heart!
Today as we near the end of our second week, I want us to discover
how the New Testament can also help us discover even more of the
Prequel, through the way this grown up baby acts and speaks,
fulfilling the ancient prophecies.

We've already considered some of those prophecies this week,
working back from their fulfilment, as the risen Christ joins the two
disappointed disciples on the road to Emmaus. Two Christmassy
links lead us to the wise men, and to Simeon when Mary and Joseph
bring their six week old son to the temple.

. . .

Let's consider the wise ones following a star. When they stop at Herod's palace to ask the way, the scribes easily find the Prequel. In the prophecy of Micah there is the reference we hear in many Carol services. It's Micah 5.2, well worth finding in your bible, because in Micah's prophecies you will also find many other references to the promised Messiah. Bear in mind that prophets 'see' in 3D – both the immediate and the far ahead, both the physical and the spiritual.

And what about that star?

Take a moment to read a couple of sentences from Numbers 24.17. You may remember Balaam as the prophet with the talking donkey? He is more than that. He is an honest and very courageous prophet, willing to challenge the command to curse the incoming people of Israel. We are told the words of his fourth oracle, prefixed by establishing his determination only to follow the words and will of God, whatever the personal consequences. (Verses 15 and 16.) He then pronounces:

"I see him but not now; I behold him, but not near. A star will come out of Jacob; a sceptre will rise out of Israel."

This prophecy, together with their knowledge of what the heavens revealed, was strong enough evidence for the wise men to embark on that long and arduous journey which eventually led them to a baby in Bethlehem.

And what of Simeon?

Luke tells us that God's Spirit had already prepared him for meeting the Messiah, so that somehow he recognised the significance of this baby. Read this passage attentively and you'll see how he foretells the necessary suffering, both of the baby in his arms, and for Mary, the baby's mother. Luke 2.25-35.

Try this...

- Have another go at memorising a sentence from scripture which means a lot to you.
- Here are some more prophecies and their fulfilment for you to check out:
- *Prophecy - Fulfilment*
- Isaiah 59.20-21 - Jesus' teaching and life
- Isaiah 61.1 - Luke.4.16-21 (particularly verse 21)
- Joel 2.28-32 - The coming of the Holy Spirit, and the crucifixion

WEEK 3: CAST LIST

MARY, JOSEPH, JOHN, GABRIEL, A SHEPHERD, JESUS

This week's prayer:
You may find it helpful to pray this prayer
each day during the third week in Advent

Jesus
> *As I watch the Christmas story,*
> *Told once more this year,*
> *Help me to catch a glimpse*
> *Of what was happening here.*
> *Help me see,*
> *behind the scripts,*
> *The wonder and the love*
> *That brought all heaven*
> *Close to earth,*
> *And earth to heaven above.*
> *Amen*

DAY 1

Reflection for Week 3, Day 1

There are plenty of plays and carol services as we get closer to Christmas. During the past two weeks we have been considering both how the life and even the suffering of Jesus had been foretold, and also that his necessary suffering ties up with our Advent realisation. If God was truly to come among us, sharing the darkness of our suffering was inevitable. The light of the world could only be real light if that Light was so loving that it was ready to take part in our darkness too.

So this week, as we start singing the carols and watching the plays, we are going to look at some of the cast in them. I'm hoping that we'll be able to understand, through them, a little more about the baby in the manger and the adult on the cross.

· · ·

We start with Mary. You remember how her cousin Elizabeth greeted her when Mary came to visit this older relative who was already six months pregnant? One of the things Elizabeth said, (I imagine with much feeling!) is what we can read in Luke 1.45: 'Blessed is she who has believed what the Lord has said to her will be accomplished!' No doubt Elizabeth was contrasting Mary's acceptance with her own husband's doubt, which had resulted in his frustrating inability to speak until John was born.

This quality in Mary is later echoed by Jesus in his response to a woman in the crowd who was focusing on the physical mothering by Mary. (Luke 11.27-28) Jesus shifts her attention to understand the far more important quality in Mary. It is, rather, her willingness to hear the word of God and obey it. In other words, her 'Yes'.

In the same way, this quality in Mary is broadened to include, as family, all who, like Mary, hear God's word and put it into practice (Luke 8.19-21). We see it, too, in what Mary says to the servants at the wedding in Cana: 'Do whatever he tells you'. John 2.1-8 Often we read this without realising its significance. The servants are surely being guided to do the same thing : to hear God's word and put it into practice.

So maybe this can remind us all to focus less on the physical, whether that be in health, childbearing, comfort or wealth, and rather to focus on what is really more important: learning to hear God's word and put it into practice. It is after all, not our will but God's will we pray for whenever we pray the Our Father.

Try this...

- Throughout today, whenever you remember, honestly and attentively pray this longing in the Lord's Prayer:
- *THY will be done!*

DAY 2

Reflection for Week 3, Day 2

The next person we are considering in the Cast of the Nativity, is Joseph. Although in many classic paintings Joseph was shown in the shadows – playing more of a walk-on role than a speaking part – he is in fact a hugely important actor in this cosmic drama of the Incarnation, as the Great Unseen Spirit God is earthed and made visible in a human life.

Like both Zachariah and Mary, Joseph is also given direct Godly guidance, to which, like Mary, he responds and obeys without hesitation. Even when this runs counter to what he has already thoughtfully decided to do about divorcing Mary quietly, he lays his own decision aside and obeys what he has been told, taking Mary as his wife. We know that a woman could be stoned to death for suspected infidelity, so Joseph was putting his own respectability and hers in jeopardy, but he doesn't hesitate. And when Herod was planning to kill the toddler Jesus, Joseph is the one to take his family by night on that dangerous journey to the safety of another country. Joseph's part in this drama is full of danger, threat, anxiety, risk and self sacrifice. Plenty of darkness, then. Yet there is also light.

Clearly, Joseph knows he can trust God. We know he is a distant descendant of King David, who also trusted God. We know he is a Bethlehem man. We know he was already engaged to Mary. So through Joseph, all those prophecies are about to be fulfilled. And once again, we find the world's Light sharing in our places of darkness.

Joseph is given the honour, not only of naming the child, but also of nurturing him. His fatherly raising of Jesus, together with Mary's mothering, will be for the growing Jesus an earthly model of God's parenting. The Holy Family needs all three people.

Try this...

- Be attentive to Joseph as you read the familiar events in Matthew 1.18-25 and then Matthew 2.13-23.

DAY 3

Reflection for Week 3, Day 3

The third person we are considering is John, son of Zachariah and Elizabeth, close relative to Mary and only six months older than Jesus. In the gospels we see John both as a baby and an adult. His name was obviously significant, as it would have been normal to have named him Zachariah, like his father. Since the Hebrew form of John (Johanan) means 'Yahweh has been gracious', we can see why the name of this promised child proclaims his mission. You can also hear its meaning as Zachariah prophesies about his son in his joy. It's in Luke 1.76-79, and is said or sung every day at morning prayer. In fact this entire prophetic song expounds on the name Zachariah has been told to give his child.

As 'Yahweh-Has-Been-Gracious' grows up, we find him seeking God in the desert, before becoming yet another fulfilled prophecy! He is Isaiah's 'Voice crying in the wilderness', doing exactly what

Zachariah had prophesied about him – going before the Lord to prepare the way for him, giving people the working knowledge about salvation by experiencing God's forgiveness.

Even in his own rejection, arrest, and execution, John's life continues the prophecy about Jesus, so John the Baptiser is a very significant player in this cosmic drama. He even baptises Jesus, publicly announcing that he himself is not the Messiah but his mission is to prepare the way for Messiah.

John has a great deal to teach us. He never points to himself, but to Jesus. In the desert he learnt attentiveness to God, wherever that led.

It did not lead him to a life of comfort and luxury, however, and the darkness of Herod's dungeon did not disappear, nor the clever cruelty of Herod's wife, Herodias, who tricked her husband into allowing John's execution.

Following Jesus involves quite a lot of darkness. In fact Jesus never sugared the pill. We are to pick up our cross – our method of execution - and follow him, Jesus said. Follow him to what? To death!

This is certainly a hard saying for us, and it's understandable that we often draw the line at accepting it. Yet terrifying as it is, Jesus knows that such commitment will actually set us free from the self-centred and allow God- centred light to shine in our hearts, healing both us and those we meet.

. . .

Try this...

- Try to learn some more about attentiveness. Whatever you are doing today use it as your practical homework. Allow the Holy Spirit to lead you deeper into your own mission, as you become more attuned to God's leading. Don't discount anything or anyone.

DAY 4

Reflection for Week 3, Day 4

Today we turn our attention to Gabriel, who has appeared to Zachariah in the temple, to Mary at home, and to Joseph in dreams. When Jesus is born and laid in a manger, it will be the angel of the Lord and a whole crowd of other angels who will appear to some Bethlehem shepherds at work in the night.

Interestingly I find that many who find it unnecessary to consider God a reality are very comfortable with angels. Angels seem to have slipped into an acceptable zone which excludes anything religious! So what kind of being is Gabriel and why are we thinking about Gabriel together now?

One reason is that Gabriel links the prequel to the present. This spirit presence has been appearing throughout the Old Testament and is clearly different from our time-bound life and death perception. In the gospel appearances Gabriel has not aged from those previous times. Angels, then, must be in a different dimension from ourselves. In Psalm 8 the psalmist marvels that humans are made 'little lower than the angels'.

There are plenty of Christian and post Christian pictures of angels, which bear little resemblance to those described in the bible. But of course all images are symbolic and we don't have to take them literally. What we do need to notice is when and why they appear, and clearly Gabriel's role is that of personal messenger. This heavenly spirit is always sent by God to tell a highly important message to someone on earth. Maybe it's such a personal message that no other means of communication is possible. Sometimes the recipient is fast asleep, as Joseph was.

The Great Spirit of God can and does speak straight into our hearts, even bypassing words. How wonderful it would be if, this new Christian year, you and I become so attuned to God's reality that we are attentive enough to receive the messages God wants us to hear. Or rather, simply to know, deep in our being, what we are to do or say.

Try this...

- Go and sit outside (wearing weather-appropriate clothing!)
- Sitting still and attentive is the only way to see wildlife. And we need a similar stillness for this. "Be still... and know... that I am God." Psalm 46.10

DAY 5

Reflection for Week 3, Day 5

As we reflect on the Nativity cast members this week, we come now to one of the shepherds. When I walked from Nazareth to Bethlehem I was surprised to see that while the town is on a hill, Shepherds Fields is below the town. So they would have run uphill to see the baby in the manger. A change of perspective so often helps us notice things differently.

Once again, in thinking of a shepherd, we find prophecies being fulfilled. In the David and Goliath event, it was this young shepherd's experience in using stones and a sling to protect his sheep that enabled him to be such a good shot. (1 Samuel 17.34-50). No doubt our shepherd used similar methods to protect his sheep.

· · ·

We are told that the shepherds were terrified when the familiar sky was suddenly bright with heavenly light. The angel of the Lord may well have been Gabriel, sent once again from heaven to give these shepherds an important message, and to reassure them in their fear. Whatever they saw, however they heard it, their initial fear turns to attentive wonder. It is clear enough to make them understand – perhaps in a new way – that the promised and expected Saviour, the Messiah, has been born. And not born in some distant place, or even in Jerusalem, but in their own local town.

When the angel calls Bethlehem the City of David we can imagine how a Bethlehem shepherd might have felt! After all, David had also been a shepherd in Bethlehem, and maybe our shepherd, too, would have always felt a special link with King David, and now be bursting with joy and pride that things had come full circle. Even heaven had let them know, in the dark of their fields, with their work clothes on, and their sheep nearby. We hear the story so often that it's easy for us to miss the staggering shock of this event. Its incredible surge of joy and excitement. The light of heaven in the physical darkness.

The angel does not give them precise instructions, nor does a star lead them (as often happens in our plays). No, the heavenly light has come instead into their hearts and minds, urging them to make their own way to Bethlehem and search for this baby in a manger. Perhaps we are reminded of those two disciples in Emmaus, saying excitedly to each other as they set off quickly to Jerusalem, "didn't our hearts burn within us?!"

And that is what this shepherd can teach us on our Advent journey. When we suddenly realise the extraordinary truth of what has happened in Jesus, how it all links up, and what a difference it makes to normality, we too find ourselves fired up – our hearts burning within us, as we set off at once into the rest of our life.

Try this...

- Read again this part of Luke's gospel. As you read, imagine being there. You may like to read it by the light of a fire. You may want to paint it, or write it as a poem or script.

DAY 6

Reflection for Week 3, Day 6

Our final cast member to think about this week is the newly born baby. Hopefully our reflections on those other members of the cast have already helped to lead us through the darkness to this small and very ordinary place. And what shall we find?

In the first week of Advent we reflected on the way Jesus comes right into our places of darkness, bringing light, certainly, but sharing our darkness too. And in the second week we dug around in prophesies and fulfilment, to discover a little more about who this child is.

Now we are ready to creep into this stabling place and look into the manger. A human baby is lying there. Mary and Joseph are there, probably very tired, and very relieved. There is always hope in the birth of a new human. There is wonder too. But a group of shepherds may be the last thing they were expecting!

For us, knowing both Prequel and Sequel, this is a highly charged moment, which is why the church has given so much significance to it. We are witnessing the Incarnation, the earthing of God. This baby, sharing our human life - even being born, and dependent - is also divine.

We know how his earthly life will end. We know that even death will not hold him. We know that although this birth happened over two thousand years ago, Jesus is still very much alive and actively involved with you and me. Having spoken all creation into being, this Word of God now speaks light and love into all life.

Try this...

- As you sing carols this Advent, don't just sing them on autopilot! Sing them as if for the first time.

WEEK 4: CURIOUS HOPE

This week's prayer:
You may find it helpful to pray this prayer each day during the fourth week in Advent

Great Spirit of God
I want to settle in stillness
And wait for you.
May nothing distract me
From attending to you.
I want to become
more and more like you -
For your love to shine through me
For your ideas to come into my mind
For your compassion to fill my heart.
Amen

DAY 1

Reflection for Week 4, Day 1

We now move into the last week of Advent, and I know this is inevitably a very busy time for many of us. I hope that the reflections this week will provide you with daily pockets of space.

I suppose the elephant in the kitchen is this: what is the point of Jesus sharing our darkness unless our darkness can completely vanish in God's light?

Maybe all the Christmas lights at this dark season of the year (in the northern hemisphere) are part of the way we pretend what we long for, with artificial lights which we pack away as soon as Christmas Day is over. But pretend light and celebration can make the reality of our darkness worse, not better. The more secular and frantic the festival becomes, the less joyful it will be. Worry, stress, finances, overwork, family conflicts. Where is the Hope in all this?

Each day this week we can be curious about the real kind of Hope!

Today's real Hope is in what the baby in the manger shows us very clearly: that God is fully, really, unreservedly, messily Here With Us. It's also Jesus's promise, when he grows up, is executed, and emerges into new life. He promises, "I am with you Always...". Matthew 28.19-20

Think about it. Imagine you are in a place so dark you have no idea how to walk safely. If the lights are switched on, you suddenly see there are all kinds of impossibly tricky obstacles around you. Are those obstacles only there in the light? Of course not! And does the light make them go away? No. But if someone comes to guide you carefully through this tangle of obstacles, then even if the obstacles are still there, you can get safely through.

It is out of Love that God becomes a human being. Out of love God promises to be with you always. The light of God's affectionate love for you doesn't necessarily make the troubles vanish. The real gift to us is God's presence, which actually makes all the difference because love takes away fear. It changes us and enables us. It sets us free.

Try this...

- Today every time you go from one room to another, and from one place to another, let the doorways remind you of this fact:
- Jesus is with you. Now. Always.
- Let this become a habit, so not just today, but every day.

DAY 2

Reflection for Week 4, Day 2

St Paul explained hope as being what you feel about something you're expecting but haven't yet got. (Romans 8.24-25) And there's plenty of that in Advent, with the lumpy wrapped parcels under the tree, and presents you ordered online but are still waiting for even though Christmas is coming alarmingly close.

When Jesus had been meeting people for forty days after the resurrection, he returned to the dimension of heaven, telling the disciples to go and wait for the gift of the Holy Spirit. That time of waiting would only have been full of hope for the disciples on one condition. They needed to take Jesus at his word. To trust what Jesus had said. And it was over a week that they had to wait!

. . .

Our hope is curious because it's unusual. Rather than the straightforward Christmas waiting until the day comes and the gift wrapping can finally be torn off, so you can hold the present you had been hoping for, Christian Hope is more like a voucher. It is both for now and for the future. Except of course it's far better than a voucher because you get to use it straight away. Perhaps it's more like receiving the latest Virtual Reality game, which you can enjoy straight away. But later, through playing, you discover that it includes a ticket to actually visit the very landscape you've been exploring!

The 'now' part of this wonderful Christian Hope is the actual presence of Jesus spiritually with you every moment of your life. As it says in so many hymns, and here in 'Lead us Heavenly Father':

> Spirit of our God descending
> Fill our hearts with heavenly joy.
> Love with every passion blending
> Pleasure that can never cloy.
> Thus Provided, Pardoned, Guided,
> Nothing can our peace destroy!

And what about the 'not yet' part of this Hope?

Well, if this lifelong Spirit presence with us is the preparation and training ground for what is still to come, we're looking at something promised beyond the limits of our earthbound life. We're talking about the dimension of Heaven.

Try this...

- Keep going with acknowledging the reality of God's Spirit right there with you wherever you go. Psalm 121 describes it very well.
- Work on enlarging your perception and attentiveness throughout the day. Realise God's presence in the queues and traffic. Look at people's faces remembering that God loves them too. Become more in tune with God's love and compassion. Remember how he had such compassion on the crowds who had made their way all round the lake to see him.

DAY 3

Reflection for Week 4, Day 3

Remember the crowds who made their journeys to Buckingham Palace to catch even a glimpse of the Queen at her platinum jubilee? Or the crowds at Glastonbury so happy to gather and wait for their favourite bands? Their Hope kickstarted their action. And that hope came from a conviction that their action would definitely be worthwhile.

It's the same with this curious hope we have as Christians. Although we can't actually see Jesus at the moment, we can meet him through the accounts of his life in the gospels, through those Bethlehem shepherds, through Mary, through Joseph, through the wise travellers following the stars, and through the bubbly excitement of his amazed followers in the Letters of Paul, Peter, John and others. But that's not all.

· · ·

Since we know that Jesus rose from certain death on Good Friday to resurrection life on the first Easter Sunday morning, we know beyond doubt that Jesus is as alive now as he was then. Alive in such a way that time and place no longer limit his presence. All we need to do is to know that, and act on it. We call it faith, only that's a word which has shifted sometimes to mean 'make believe'. As if God, like Santa, only exists if we choose to believe in him. But curiously this isn't make believe. It's real! Perhaps a better word would be one describing what the crowds at the lake, and the crowds at the Palace and at Glastonbury centre stage all knew. They all had no doubt about it. They were all convinced that their Hope was worthwhile, based on their experience.

Let's listen to something else Jesus said. It's in Luke 4.34. "For where your treasure is, there your heart will be also." And after Jesus had restored the sight of a blind man, who had consequently been driven out by the religious leaders, John tells us, 'Jesus heard that they had driven him out, and when he found him, he said, "Do you believe in the Son of Man?" He answered, "And who is he, sir? Tell me, so that I may believe in him." Jesus said to him, "You have SEEN him, and the one speaking with you is he." He said, "Lord, I believe." And he worshipped him.' John 9.35-38.

Try this...

- Call to mind how you felt when first you realised that what you had thought was 'make believe' was actually true. And if that hasn't happened yet, consider the possibility that it is true, and you can know it after all.

DAY 4

Reflection for Week 4, Day 4

Another reason the Christian hope is curious, is that it encompasses more than our dimension of time. Mostly people take it for granted that reality only applies to what we can see or measure. The material, the physical. But that is quite a narrow way of thinking, and many people catch glimpses of a wider understanding, realising that although matter matters and is full of surprises, full reality doesn't stop there. Full reality is wider, deeper and way beyond our understanding.

And yet it's also utterly and beautifully simple. After all, we don't need to grasp how a computer works in order to use it. The prayer Jesus gave us is simple enough to use and yet profound enough to touch both our needs and God's love.

· · ·

So our hope is grounded in what Jesus shows us of God. And it is true both now, during our universe-locked existence, and also in the wide, bright space of the heavenly. The good, the loving, the serving and caring which develop and accumulate during our lives, bring us ever closer to the loving heart of God. This means that when death comes to us it won't be annihilation or nothingness, but new resurrection life, as we are permanently enfolded in that loving heart of God.

Jesus taught us about it, explained that he was the Way to it, and even demonstrated it in his own post-death life, meetings, conversations and actions.

We are assured by the resurrected Jesus, that we too can share in this Hope.

Try this...

- It's very likely that you will be hearing or singing more carols this week! Remember to notice their message of hope. Like this verse from O Little Town of Bethlehem:

How silently, how silently The wondrous gift is given!
So God imparts to human hearts The blessings of his heaven.
No ear may hear his coming But in this world of sin
Where meek souls will receive him
Still the dear Christ enters in.

DAY 5

Reflection for Week 4, Day 5

Christina Rossetti's poem *In the bleak midwinter* is an imaginative reflection on the Nativity. The words 'bleak', 'moan', 'hard as iron' immediately put us in touch with the areas of life which are numbingly bleak, desolate, cold and dark. And it is into this landscape that the pent up love of God bursts in all its fullness.

But like a huge orchestra playing very softly and tenderly, Rossetti shows the loving humility of God, with simple earthly things becoming lit up with such Godly humility. This breaking into God's own creation by the Creator shows no sign of pomposity or disdain. Instead, we watch the real hope of the Incarnation as it happens – full of courtesy, respect and appreciation, exactly what Jesus showed as he, their lord and master, knelt and washed his disciples' feet.

. . .

The final verse of this poem explores what we have been reflecting on. Real hope galvanises action. And the poet is at a loss to know what on earth can match such love. Only one thing is both necessary and possible, but so hard. We can only do the same: 'give my heart'.

But, strangest of wonders and wonderfully strange, when we reach this point of giving our selves, we actually find that God enables us to be more our true selves than ever! Maybe the angels laugh as well as singing whenever it happens. However many times it happens during a person's life. The journey to find Jesus may indeed be hard and the way steep. But always we are being guided, whether we realise it or not. And always the door is open and suddenly we kneel in worship.

Try this...

- Read the words of this carol as the poem it is, and let the words lead you back to Christina Rossetti's thinking as she wrote it.
- As you decorate or bake in preparation for Christmas, make them a spiritual preparation as well.

DAY 6

Reflection for Week 4, Day 6

And so we have come full circle on this Advent journey. We began with Darkness and we end with Light. We have focused on the importance of Jesus, the light, coming to share our darkness, and discovered how Hope encompasses both the present, sharing our darkness here with us, and also the full light of heaven which is still to come.

We have engaged with the past, as Prequel, the present, as Presence, and now the future, which you might think of as the Sequel! A sequel which hasn't yet happened for us, and for which we hope. We don't hope for it in the sense of wishful thinking, but in the sense of anticipating what we know will take place, just like those crowds at the lakeside, in front of the Palace and around the Glastonbury stage.

. . .

Enjoying the fulfilment of God's promise in our life here, is what liberates us to be the person God loves into being. With all our colours and characters bright, we can walk in both darkness and light together, always accompanied and buoyed up by the One who knows us better than we know ourselves and loves us so much.

What an adventure each day becomes! What a pilgrimage each lifetime becomes. As we stand on the Advent foothills of this year, can we commit ourselves to walking through each season in the company of this earthed God who was born as a baby and laid in a manger because there was no room in the inn.

Try this...

- Set a nativity scene in your home, or create one, and use it as a focus for worship.
- Christ is in Christmas already! All we need to do is remember God's love whenever and wherever we are.

An Advent Reflection to finish with.

In the darkness of night when space displays its distances
Marked by the light of each star
We can stand on the earth and wonder at infinity
Stretching amazingly far.
And now the Maker of all things, Lord of the universe
Out of love becomes what God has made
And here in a manger, newly born and very small
Jesus our Saviour is laid.

On the rough stable floor the shepherds kneel and worship him.
Unseen, the angels adore.
By the light of a lamp his mother Mary nurses him
Joseph holds open the door.
And though our journey to find him has covered weary miles
In such joy all weariness will fade
For here in a manger, newly born and very small
Jesus our Saviour is laid.